DEAL WITH IT

ABLEISM

DEAL WITH IT AND APPRECIATE EVERYONE'S ABILITIES

Written by Kimberly Maich

Illustrated by Kay Nau

James Lorimer & Company Ltd., Publishers
Toronto

Contents

"That's so lame." Caleb's eyes shifted to the sound of his new classmate's voice and then down to the crutch. He felt like he had been using it forever — and he probably would use it forever.

"Do you even know what that word means?" He found himself cringing.

"Nobody cares," his classmate responded, "but low-key pathetic! Like you."

This book helps explain what ableism is, what it targets, facts about it, and how to recognize and respond to it in your everyday life. You'll learn about disabled students that are the targets of ableism, the language around ableism, students' rights, and the barriers the world puts up that make it even harder for people with disabilities to navigate.

Ableist people include those who upset others with their ableist thoughts, words, actions — even humour that hurts. Let's explore what ableism is and how it impacts our lives.

WHAT IS ABLEISM?

Ableism is the idea that what we think of as "normal" is better than not being normal. It's a kind of discrimination against disability. Ableism can target our bodies, minds, and even our culture as not good enough or not worth enough. Ableism can be personal (just about us), but it can also be much bigger, as part of larger systems like the schools we go to every day.

Ableism is . . .

- Name-calling about someone's body and mind.
- Making fun of someone for not doing something better or faster.
- Leaving someone out because of their body or mind.
- Forcing everyone to do things the same way.
- Insisting that everyone's bodies should be the same.
- Believing everyone's minds or brains should be the same.
- Teasing someone for doing something differently.
- Judging all parts of someone because of one part of them.
- Believing all people with a certain feature are a certain way.
- Thinking that someone who is disabled is not capable, skilled, or smart.
- Thinking that "normal" is better or that everyone should be that way.
- Believing people with disabilities don't belong with their families.

It is also taking away . . .

- Someone's help because you don't think they need it.
- Someone's help because you think they should do it themselves.
- Someone's voice.
- Someone's tools (such as a wheelchair, walker, or crutches) because you think they're embarrassing.
- Spaces set aside to make disabled lives better (like a parking spot or a seat on a bus).

ABLEISM TARGETS:

BODIES

IF YOU DON'T HAVE TWO LEGS AND TWO ARMS AND TWO EYES (YOU GET THE PICTURE), YOU AREN'T GOOD ENOUGH.

MINDS

IF YOU USE ASSISTIVE TECHNOLOGY TO EXPRESS YOUR VOICE, WHAT YOU'RE DOING DOESN'T COUNT.

RELATIONSHIPS

YOU SHOULD ONLY SPEND TIME WITH PEOPLE LIKE YOURSELF.

RIGHTS

YOU'RE RESTRICTED FROM PARTICIPATING IN GROUP ACTIVITIES BECAUSE OF YOUR DISABILITY.

QUIZ: ABLEISM OR NOT?

Ableism is felt throughout society. Sometimes it's on purpose, and sometimes it's not. But it makes disabled lives harder in so many ways. See if the following examples are ableism — or not!

1. Is faster always better?

Yehor gets teased every sports day. He has cerebral palsy, but nobody knows this about him. It means he can't run well or quickly on the track.

It's probably unintentional personal ableism. Even his friends don't know about his difficulties with movement. Think before you tease!

2. Ads "R" Us — or are they?

Caleb notices the social media ads for his health care clinic not only feature mostly white males, but also lack evident bodily differences in any of the pictures.

This is an example of intentional ableism in the media, where ads might avoid showing disability.

3. You don't belong here.

Rosa's neighbour called a social worker on her. The social worker agrees with the neighbour that because of Rosa's son's behaviour problems, he or her daughters should be placed in a different home.

This is ableism, which affects how families are treated by community members or professionals, even when it comes to behaviour. Families should be supported, not separated.

4. You should be like me.

Eva's friends told her that she should put a napkin over her prosthetic hand at lunch.

Ableism can happen because friends think that what is considered "normal" is better. Nobody should have to hide a disability to fit in — especially with their friends.

5. *To work or not to work?*

Albert really wanted to apply for a job at a store stocking shelves, but the ad said he had to lift fifty pounds.

This is ableism in the workplace. His employer could easily find ways to adapt.

6. *Bad at math?*

Jo is what they call "bad at math" or even "super-bad at math." They use an app, a calculator, and a big binder of flowcharts to help.

This behaviour doesn't sound like ableism — it sounds like an accommodation, which means that more tools are needed to help learn math. But it's even better if anyone can use them when they need them.

7. *If you don't talk, you don't think.*

Zoe uses a tablet and an app to speak, but lots of people assume she can't think at all because she doesn't use words out loud.

It's definitely ableism to believe one part of your body or your behaviour means other things too — or that using a device as part of your voice isn't good enough.

8. *Run, walk, or roll — or not?*

Francis wanted to enter the five-kilometre event and hoped to win a medal. But the organizers wouldn't let them register and said only running or walking counts for medals.

This rule or policy is an example of ableism. Our bodies are not all the same, and they don't have to do the same things. All participation must be welcome — and count.

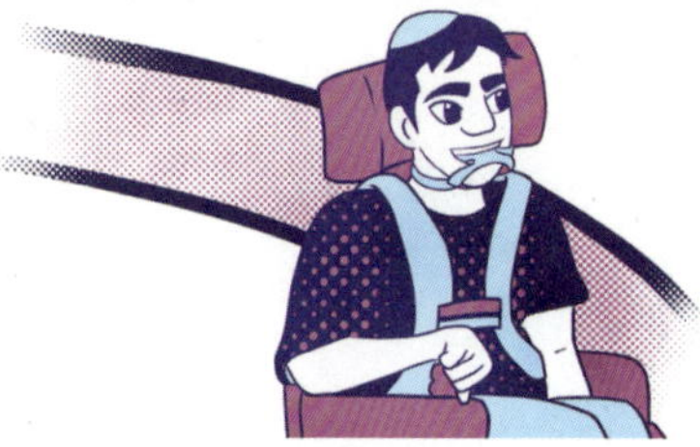

9. *A+*

The office displays projects that get an A+. Noelle is embarrassed her projects are never there.

This issue could be ableism if it's related to a disability. Ableism can be part of a big system like schools. Sometimes we don't notice it because it's been going on for so long. We need to celebrate all bodies, all minds, and all projects!

10. *Suffering.*

Lukas keeps hearing people say he "suffers" from diabetes when they see him leave the classroom to inject insulin privately.

Telling someone they suffer from anything is definitely ableism. We can't know what someone else is feeling, and we can't assume that someone else is suffering.

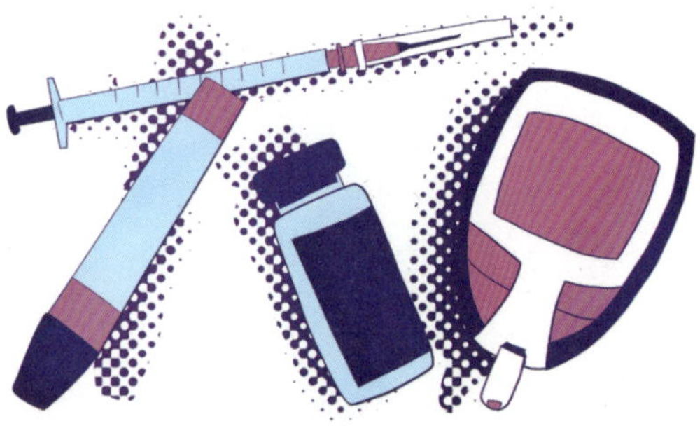

DEAR CONFLICT COUNSELLOR

Q: I get really uncomfortable when friends use words that seem to hurt other people rather than help. They don't seem to get in trouble with teachers, maybe because these words aren't swears. Does that mean it's okay? For example, they love calling people "spazzes."

A: Definitely not okay. As a society, we mostly seem to understand now that calling someone the "r-word" is not okay. Sometimes people will ask the other person to stop using such language, or will correct the person when a word like this is used. Maybe your teachers do this. But other times. people go under the radar and use words that mean almost the same thing, like "spaz." Some people don't know the history of the words they use and what they mean — they're just trying to hurt and insult. But they're doing it through ableism, and they probably don't even realize it. That doesn't make it okay. Words change over time, and the meanings and feelings that go with them change too.

Q: In science class, I was doing one of the experiments I invented, but not the one my teacher asked us to do because that one was too easy. (I'm autistic, by the way.) So, I did this really awesome experiment that made stuff expand and fly up toward the ceiling. Then my lab partner packed up her textbook and went and sat at a different table. She said, "Your brain is definitely missing some parts. You're definitely not normal. You're crazy. I'm out."

A: When your classmate is uncomfortable about the differences in your knowledge and skill and tries to bring you down, it sounds like ableism. It sounds like your classmate is trying to pick on your unique brain and use it as an insult to cover discomfort.

Q: Is it okay for my friend's mom to say that I can't come to a sleepover because it's too hard to get me upstairs where the bunk beds are?

A: No. She should figure out a different way to make sleepovers work for everyone. If the stairs in the house make it difficult for you, then how about a sleepover in the living room? It's a lot of fun to snooze in sleeping bags on the floor and couches if that means that all friends can be together.

MYTHS

If a person can't do things the way they are asked or the way it seems everyone else does them, it's not good enough.

Everyone has different ways of doing things — sometimes in ways you can't even see. Being supportive of the different ways people do stuff is the right thing to do.

Disabled people can leave their devices at home sometimes.

Devices help disabled people. When disabled people don't have their devices, they can't do what they usually can. Disabled people have the right to move and communicate at all times.

Disabled people are inspiring.

Disabled people are probably just living their lives. They might not be interested in being someone's inspiration.

Kids in my class who are disabled can't do things.

Disability doesn't mean a person can't do things. More often, it means the world around them makes it difficult to do things.

If someone can't talk to me the "regular way," that's not my problem.

It's our job to be caring with everyone, and that includes caring if other people can communicate with you. You can talk and listen with a digital voice, with sign language, and more!

People should be independent and do things all on their own.

Everyone is dependent on someone else for some things. They might be big things or little things, but we all need other people.

We don't have to change the way we do things.

If we leave people out, we do have to change things. Instead of planning a running event, we can plan one with different ways to join like walking, strolling, rolling, and more.

Disabled bodies are always seen with the eyes.

We can't always see disabled bodies. Things that give people clues about disability might be under our clothes, in places that people can't see, or are simply something that can never be seen with our eyes, no matter how hard we might try.

ABLEISM AND ME

"Blind this, blind that, blind everything," Jude grumbled. "Seriously? If we want to cover something up, it's blinded. If something is hiding, it's blind. If we don't understand something, we are blind to it. It makes my brain hurt so much that every bad thing in the world seems to be labelled as blind — without anybody even thinking about it."

Q: I need an assistive writing program for class. The school's version doesn't work the way I need it to. I was told the newer version doesn't fit their budget.

Assistive tech exists to level the playing field between disabled and non-disabled students. It helps students do their work well and quickly. This helps you academically, and the point of school is learning and success. Sometimes budgets seem to show something is too expensive when only one person may need it. But nobody needs stuff that doesn't work well. And technology could help other students too.

Q: If I have to hear I "have" autism spectrum disorder one more time, I'm gonna have a meltdown. I "am" autistic. Why can't people understand that's my identity?

Person-first language has been around for a long time, which means mentioning the person first and the disability second. That's why you will hear phrases like "student with autism."

There's a new awakening to disability identity and pride, and now many people (like you) choose to use identity-first language, which means that the disability is part of the person's identity and culture. Let people know that you prefer identity-first language!

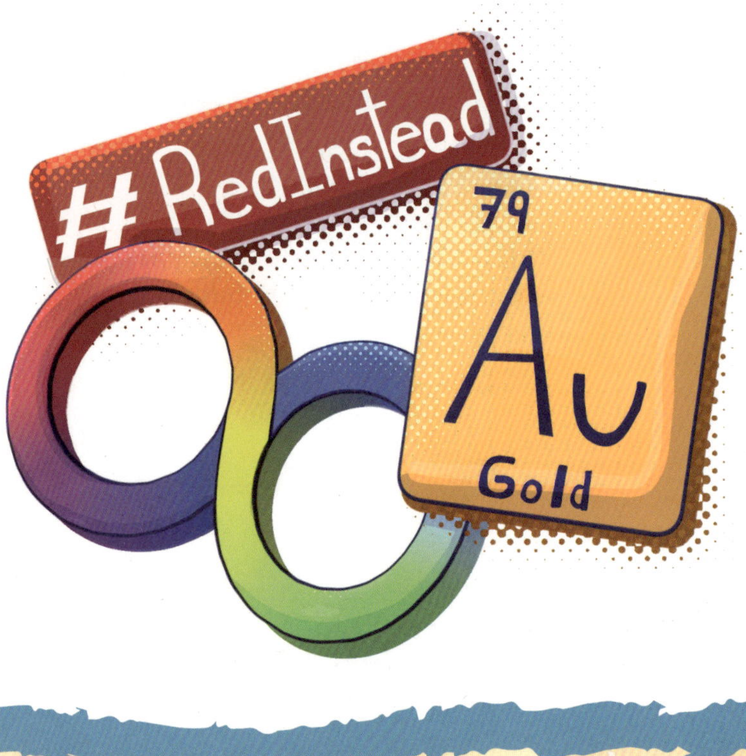

IS THE PROBLEM YOU — OR IS IT THE WORLD?

When a disabled person encounters something that is difficult to navigate because of their disability, we have two options. We can either think of the disabled person as the main issue, or we can think of the barriers the world puts up as the main issue. Seeing the disabled person as the issue might be ableism! Let's see how these attitudes look as ME problems or WORLD problems.

1. **Being told you can't be in your classroom because the lights are too bright.**
   a. A ME problem: I should have to wear sunglasses to block the light or squint when brightness starts to bother me. Right?
   b. A WORLD problem: The lights can be turned down or changed so they don't hurt my eyes. This helps other people in my classroom too.
2. **Being left behind on a school trip because nobody is available to help you get on and off the bus.**
   a. A ME problem: I should have my family take me because they know how to help. I should have a specialized lift on the school bus. Maybe I should find a part-time job so that I can pay for someone to help me?
   b. A WORLD problem: Someone should be available to help, like an adult or a friend — or even the driver. Everyone needs help at times.
3. **Not being invited to a pool party because the parents are scared a behaviour crisis will happen and they won't know what to do, or they believe they'll make problems worse.**
   a. A ME problem: I should learn not to run off when things get too stressful. I shouldn't find water so upsetting when I get wet unexpectedly. I should stop having meltdowns when things don't go the way I expect.
   b. A WORLD problem: I should explain that my family can help me on the weekends. They can help the other parents find a safe place for me if worries start getting to me. I should still be invited. Having friends and having fun is important.

4. **Not being allowed help at school because all the money is already used up for other things like pencils and books.**
    a. A ME problem: If my needs are too big, nothing can be done. If my needs happen too early or late in the year, nothing can be done. If the school helpers can't come to work, nobody else can help either.
    b. A WORLD problem: Along with my family, I should ask for help from my teachers, my principal, and the school board, and stand up for what I need. Missing support tells me more needs to be done.

WAYS TO DEAL WITH IT

You can know your own individual needs.

- Attend meetings about you and your needs and ask for things that will make you successful — like accommodations at school.

You can know your rights.

- Ask and learn about things like human rights and legislation to become aware of what your legal rights are.

You can know your freedoms.

- You are free to be yourself and to be free from problems like ableism while you go about living as a disabled person.

You can advocate for your needs.

- You have the right to advocate for yourself and to ask for what you need to live your life how you want, free from barriers.

You can learn who the helpers are in your school.

- Figure out who the kind people are and make friends with them. They will help too.

You can be direct. Again!

- Even though you might feel you have asked for support countless times, every day, you can ask again. You can be direct because some people don't get it unless you are very clear — again and again.

You can give examples.

- It can help others to understand what disability means for life every day. Someone might be able to see a scar, but they might not understand that for you that scar means you don't have enough energy to walk far on your own.

ABLEIST ACTIONS

Sometimes we say or do things and we're not sorry. Sometimes we don't (yet) get that we should be sorry until we learn a little more. Sometimes we think we're teasing gently to try to be funny, but it feels different for the other person. These things can happen with disability too. Someone in your class who is disabled might seem very different than you, but everyone can become ill, get older, or become disabled at any time in life. You could, too!

AM I ABLEIST?

1. People say I should stop using words like "crazy."
2. People tell me that I stare too much, especially if I see someone using wheels to get around.
3. If I see someone using a walker, I might grab it to help them over curbs.
4. People tell me I shouldn't keep using the accessible washroom stall.

5. I told my aunt to use my grandma's accessible parking permit because the parking lot in the mall is really busy.
6. People told me to "shush!" when I was giggling at a kid getting stuck on the stairlift.
7. People cringe at me when I say "spaz!"
8. I thought it was so funny when I asked that guy in our school with the strange lip, "Shouldn't you get that fixed?"
9. I argued with the school custodian that they should clean off the stairs first because more people use them.
10. I call my grandfather "stone deaf."
11. My teacher thinks I'm SO *NOT* funny when I use computer programs to transcribe swearing instead of writing assignments.
12. People tell me to stop when I say someone is "crippled with" anxiety.
13. People tell me my jokes go too far when I imitate people who can't walk "right."

WAYS TO DEAL WITH IT

ABLEIST NO MORE

- Listen when people give you feedback. If they say your jokes about disability are awful, your words are bad choices, or your language makes them uncomfortable, stop, think, and make some changes. Real change happens one step at a time. What ableist words can you remove from your vocabulary?
- If people say your behaviour around disability really stinks too, it's time to change. What ableist behaviour can you remove from how you act every day?
- Pay attention to your thoughts. You might catch yourself thinking when you see a disabled person, "They're just doing that to get sympathy," or "They should work on overcoming that," or "They're just lazy." Listen to your thinking, notice, and then correct it. Practice might not make perfect, but it makes things a whole lot better!

- Talk with disabled people. Have a conversation. Learn about life. Make a friend. Like you, disabled people are going about their lives. You might find out your life isn't that different, but also that it is, and you can go about the business of making things easier instead of being a pain in someone else's life.

ABLEISM PUSH-BACK

Speed is not everything.

If we're disabled, if we can't do something better and faster than someone else, and someone has a problem with that, it's probably ableism. Real life doesn't have a winner.

Let everyone do things their way.

If we're disabled and find a new or different way to do something, and if someone has a problem with that, it's likely ableism. We're allowed to do what works — our way.

You're not the boss of the world.

If someone thinks we have to do a thing one way and tries to force those ideas and ideals onto others, that person might be showing ableism. The world is full of different people doing different things in different ways. Why not just be amazed (in a good way)?

Everyone is extraordinary — not just you.

Like many things, ableism is wrapped up in power and privilege. People might think that because their clothes or their brains or their bodies are a certain way, they're more important. But they aren't worth more than you. Nobody is.

VISIBLE OR INVISIBLE?

Sometimes we talk about disabilities as something can see or not see — visible or invisible.

If someone is using an accessible parking spot, but we don't see them using a device or having trouble walking, should they be using this spot? Well, we also can't see bad arthritis in their knees or a long scar down their chest from heart surgery. Don't be the one who makes a judgement without information. Assume that people know what they need. They usually don't need anyone to judge their choices.

Differences in how various disabilities are treated can make people feel better or worse. We might jump to wrong conclusions.

Visible

Visible disabilities are ones we can easily see, like those requiring the use of prosthetic limbs, crutches, canes, wheelchairs, technology, and more.

We should be aware of how we may show more empathy and support for those with obvious disabilities.

Invisible

Invisible disabilities are those we can't see easily. They include difficulties with hearing, understanding and communicating, as well as chronic pain, and more.

We must remember that invisible disabilities are possible. Not considering them hinders our relationships with others.

ALLIES AGAINST ABLEISM

I peeked around the corner of the wall because I could hear snickering with a mean edge. I saw Amal's tiny spaceships surrounded by pylons marking them "not to be touched." They get pretty upset if anyone touches their stuff. These other kids were shoving Amal's spaceships into their pockets and tossing some over the fence. I know they know better.

WAYS TO DEAL WITH IT: DO MORE THAN IGNORE

- Be aware that some other kids or adults might be out to hurt and not help. Be the person who takes the next step and calls them out. (If you don't feel safe, privately ask another adult to help.)
- Recognize that YOU can make a difference at your school. You can be a leader in cheering for how we are all different. Celebrate what differences bring to our classroom, our community, our playground, and our world.
- If you don't know what to do, teach yourself. Join a club, start an organization, make a poster, read a book, and make changes to your whole classroom. Celebrate diversity. Celebrate all bodies.
- Be you. When you're you, you teach others how to be themselves. After you're done figuring out being you, be the change too.

ONE WORLD — TOGETHER

We live together in one world. Kids. Adults. Friends. Enemies. People who look like us or don't look like us. People who have bodies like ours — or don't. People who use technology to talk or words to talk. We all share space in the world, everywhere people go.

At some point, we get that we're not here just to help ourselves. We also need to help others. We can make change happen. When we see something that we know isn't right, like someone hiding a classmate's tablet when they use it to talk, it's okay to help. We have the power to make someone's day better, to let them know that they have a friend, and to show them that someone is going to help.

Then that other kid will know picking on someone because of their body, their technology, a disability, or a need that's just different than their own isn't okay at all. We have the power to help stop it, to turn it around, and to show other people who are watching that ableism doesn't win.

ABLEISM: YOU PROBABLY ALREADY KNOW IT WHEN IT'S HAPPENING

You know ableism exists and that it's not right. But what do you actually do when you know it's happening? This quiz has no clear right or wrong answers because every situation is unique, and you might make different choices at different times. Always try to make things better — now and later.

1. It's "Just You"

Someone tells a disabled classmate there's only one of them — and a lot of people aren't like them.

- Explain that quantity (how many) isn't more important than quality (being a real, authentic person and friend).
- Ask if that means red-haired people should also have a problem.
- Just listen and learn what not to say.

2. Want or Need?

Someone is hogging the personal workstation to chew gum without getting in trouble. It's the only desk with privacy barriers for when students are feeling down or need to work without distractions.

- Ask for your turn and then give it to someone else you know who needs it and can't study without being distracted.
- Ask your teacher to set a timer so it can be someone else's turn soon.
- Suggest that the workstation be monitored so it's used the way it should be.

3. Jokers Aren't Funny

A student uses a cane to get around when the ground is uneven in the sports field. A kid from your neighbourhood walks behind them and copies the way they move.

- Ask if they would make fun of their grandmother for using a cane.
- Approach the staff to put up anti-ableism posters.
- Remember who that student is so you can keep away from them in the future.

4. Exclusion Hurts

You see a poster advertising an event you know your friend can't go to because she has a badly broken leg.

- Email the people running the event and ask them why everyone isn't welcome.
- Just stay home with your friend and do something else to have fun another way.
- Talk to your friend and her parents and figure out a way to be helpful, flexible, and creative so she can still go to the event

5. Mean ≠ Humour

You're walking to the bathroom and see someone you don't know putting a paper over the sign for "resource room" that changes "source" to "tard."

- Take a photo of the sign and show the resource teacher or principal.
- Tear down the sign.
- Work on raising the awareness of the whole school around the "r-word."

6. Cheer Louder

At a sports event, one of the runners is much slower. A group of parents sitting in the front row of the bleachers is booing.

- Stand by the finish line, call the runner's name, and cheer loudly!
- Stand beside where the parents are booing, and cheer louder than they are cheering!
- Just turn and frown at them.

7. Let People Be Themselves

A student is laughing at someone for wearing headphones to block out the sounds of busy school hallways.

- Wear headphones to school tomorrow.
- Talk to the other kid about your own noise-cancelling earbuds.
- Tell the laughing student that nobody is laughing at his hat or his glasses and ask, "What's the difference?"

8. Devices Help Everyone

An adult comments that someone is "weird" because they're using an electronic device to shut off the lights in their house instead of using the wall switch.

- Ask that adult if they use a phone or computer for anything and how it's different.
- Explain that some people have invisible issues that might not be easily understood. That adult should think about that first.
- Think about how it's true we all need other people or things to help us every day. Not just because we might be disabled.

9. Technology Is Access

At the community centre, you see two teenagers laughing and pointing at someone using a scanning pen to help them read the text in the event pamphlet.

- Ask the two teens, "What's so funny?"
- Go and sit beside the person using the scanning pen and ask them about it.
- Stare at the bullies disapprovingly.

10. Taking Spaces

The school's relaxation station is full of other students lying on their backs with their feet up on the walls, playing games on their phones, and laughing about how they "got out of class." Other students are standing in the hallway waiting their turn, looking uncomfortable.

- Call out the students who are misusing the space.
- Alert the nearest teacher or administrator to help clear out the room for students who need it.
- Just remember those students and watch out for them bullying others — or you — in the future.

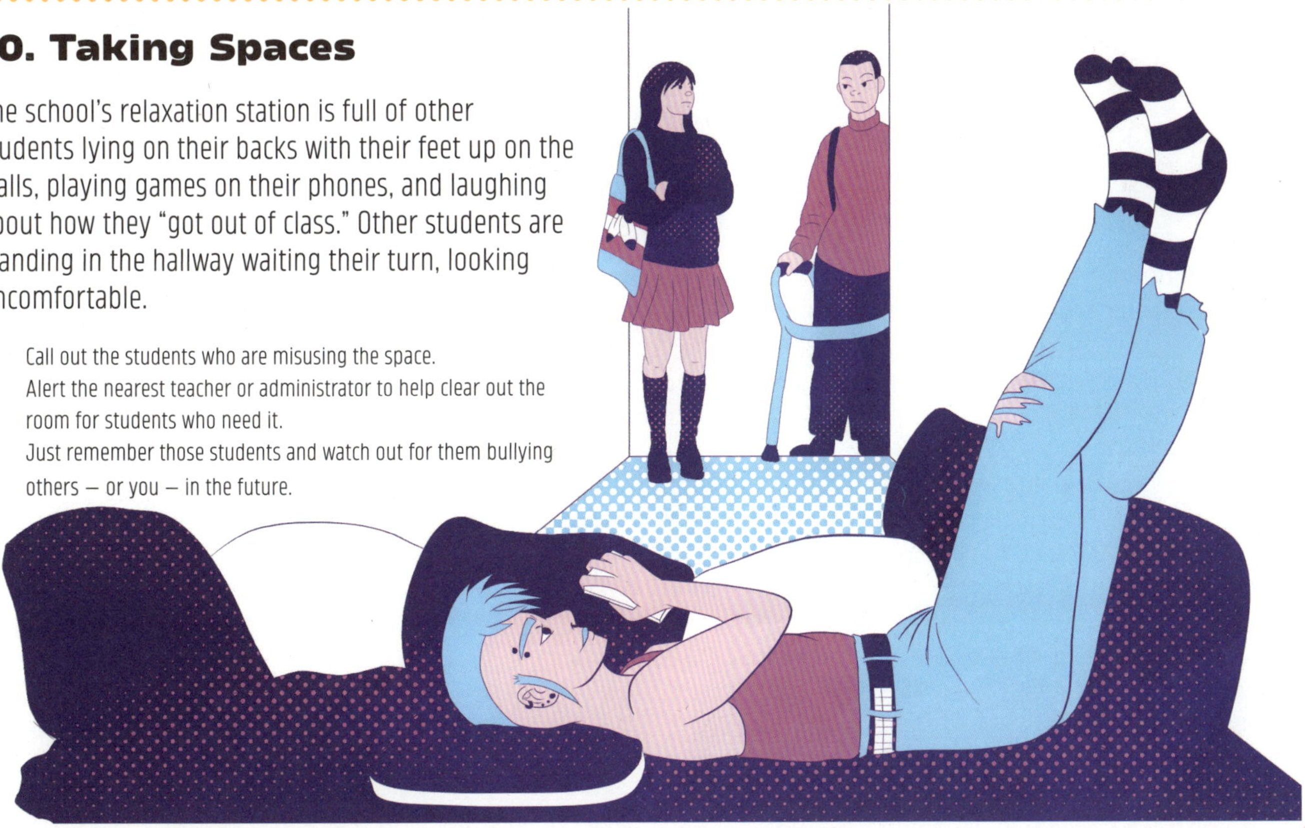

MORE HELP

Now you know a bit more about ableism. You know what it is, how it works, how it hurts others, and how you can deal with it in your everyday life. Now you can recognize it when you think it, feel it, observe it — and find ways to make the places where you live, study, and just hang out into places where disabled people face less discrimination and have better support. One person at a time.

Websites

Inclusion Canada https://inclusioncanada.ca/this-is-ableism/

Disability in Canada: Facts and Figures https://easterseals.ca/wp-content/uploads/2016/12/Disability-in-Canada-Facts-Figures.pdf

Disability Benefits: https://www.canada.ca/en/services/benefits/disability.html

Books

Disability without Labels: Looking after Louis (Ely, 2005)

Demystifying Disability: What to Know, What to Say, and How to be an Ally (Ten Speed Press, 2021)

Undoing Ableism: Teaching about Disability in K-12 Classrooms (Routledge, 2019)

Videos

This is Ableism (Inclusion Canada) https://www.youtube.com/watch?v=OdK9Av9XgjE&ab_channel=InclusionCanada

Helplines

Kids Help Phone
1-800-668-6868 or Text 686868

Organizations

Guide to Government of Canada Services for People with Disabilities and their families
https://publications.gc.ca/collections/Collection/SD18-5-2006E.pdf

Smile Canada
https://www.smilecan.org/

For help in finding Canadian books, contact the Toronto Public Library (416-393-4446 / Lillian H. Smith Branch) or, if you are a member, the Canadian Children's Book Centre (416-975-0010). The Library and Archive's Amicus and PIKA databases are available online free of charge at https://www.collectionscanada.ca

Other Titles in the Deal With It Series

Transphobia: Deal With It by j wallace skelton. Lorimer, 2016
Biphobia: Deal With It by Gordon Nore. Lorimer, 2023

Published in Canada in 2023. Published in the United States in 2023.

James Lorimer & Company Ltd., Publishers acknowledges funding support from the Ontario Arts Council (OAC), an agency of the Government of Ontario. We acknowledge the support of the Canada Council for the Arts, which last year invested $153 million to bring the arts to Canadians throughout the country. This project has been made possible in part by the Government of Canada and with the support of Ontario Creates.

Cover image: Kay Nau
Cover design: Tyler Cleroux
Series design: Tyler Cleroux

Library and Archives Canada Cataloguing in Publication
Title: Ableism : deal with it and appreciate everyone's abilities / written by Kimberly Maich ; illustrated by Kay Nau.
Names: Maich, Kimberly, 1969- author. | Nau, Kay, illustrator.
Series: Deal with it (Toronto, Ont.)
Description: Series statement: Deal with it
Identifiers: Canadiana 20230149006 | ISBN 9781459417380 (hardcover)
Subjects: LCSH: Discrimination against people with disabilities—Juvenile literature. | LCGFT: Instructional and educational works.
Classification: LCC HV1568 .M35 2023 | DDC j305.9/08—dc23

James Lorimer & Company Ltd., Publishers
117 Peter Street, Suite 304
Toronto, ON, Canada, M5V 0M3
www.lorimer.ca

Distributed in Canada by:
Formac Lorimer Books
5502 Atlantic Street
Halifax, NS, Canada
B3H 1G4
www.formaclorimerbooks.ca

Distributed in the US by:
Lerner Publisher Services
241 1st Ave. N.
Minneapolis, MN, USA
55401
www.lernerbooks.com

Printed and bound in Korea.